A man cannot help but want to teach his son everything he knows. Okay, maybe not everything but definitely the important things — the best things — the things he's learned on his own journey through life that shaped him into the best version of himself. The values, characteristics, and ethics he hopes will be the foundation of his son's life.

A father leads best by example, but often leans on sayings and quotes to impart his wisdom. Like My Dad Always Said serves to illustrate these expressions as important learning tools to not only preserve them, but to convey the importance of each and encourage conversation between a father and his son. This book is not intended to dismiss a woman's role in shaping her child, but is meant to empower men on their journey as a father to a son.

While reading this book, we hope your son asks, "What does that mean?" We encourage each father to utilize the sayings in this book as a starting point to share his own thoughts and experiences with his son that ultimately leads to insightful dialogue to shape his thinking and personal foundation.

Always carry your end of the board

Whether you
Think you can
or you Can't,
Either way
You're right

Don't cry
over
Spilt milk!

Work Hard, Play Hard.

Manners
Go A Long Way
And Don't Cost
A Dime

Never Test the Depth Of Water With Both Feet

There's always time
To do things Right
The First Time!

God gave you
Two ears
And One Mouth
So you could Listen
Twice as much
As you Talk

A little dirt
Never hurt
Anyone !

The Early Bird Gets the Worm!

Nobody Likes A Crybaby

Trust your Gut

if you
tell the Truth,
You Won't
Have to Remember
What You Said

Tell us what YOUR dad always said!

Follow us on Instagram!
@dadalwayssaid

Like us on Facebook
@dadalwayssaid

Website: www.3hbooks.com

E-mail us: share@3hbooks.com

NextGen Dad™

CPSIA information can be obtained
at www.ICGtesting.com
Printed in the USA
BVHW02*2025240818
524428BV00008B/4/P